EMMANUEL JOSEPH

The Global Architects, Billionaires, Countries, and the Blueprint for a New World Order

Copyright © 2025 by Emmanuel Joseph

All rights reserved. No part of this publication may be reproduced, stored or transmitted in any form or by any means, electronic, mechanical, photocopying, recording, scanning, or otherwise without written permission from the publisher. It is illegal to copy this book, post it to a website, or distribute it by any other means without permission.

First edition

*This book was professionally typeset on Reedsy.
Find out more at reedsy.com*

Contents

1. Chapter 1: The Dawn of Economic Titans ... 1
2. Chapter 2: Sovereign States and Economic Sovereignty ... 3
3. Chapter 3: The Digital Revolution and Global Connectivity ... 5
4. Chapter 4: Philanthropy and Global Impact ... 7
5. Chapter 5: The Influence of Media Moguls ... 9
6. Chapter 6: Environmental Stewardship and Sustainability ... 11
7. Chapter 7: The Future of Global Governance ... 13
8. Chapter 8: The Role of Financial Powerhouses ... 15
9. Chapter 9: Health and Biotechnology Innovations ... 17
10. Chapter 10: Education and Knowledge Economy ... 19
11. Chapter 11: Cultural and Creative Industries ... 21
12. Chapter 12: Space Exploration and the Final Frontier ... 23
13. Chapter 13: The Intersection of Technology and Human Rights ... 25
14. Chapter 14: Global Health Crises and Pandemic Preparedness ... 27
15. Chapter 15: The Power of Social Movements ... 29
16. Chapter 16: The Future of Work and Economic Inclusion ... 30
17. Chapter 17: Charting a New Course for the Global Future ... 32
18. Epilogue: The Legacy of the Global Architects ... 34

1

Chapter 1: The Dawn of Economic Titans

In the early 21st century, the rise of a new breed of billionaires fundamentally reshaped the global economic landscape. These individuals, emerging from diverse sectors such as technology, finance, and manufacturing, amassed unprecedented wealth, positioning themselves as influential players on the world stage. Their wealth granted them access to power corridors traditionally reserved for statesmen, allowing them to influence global policies and economic strategies. The intersection of immense personal fortune and geopolitical interests marked a shift towards a new global order, where the lines between private wealth and public power began to blur.

The influence of these billionaires extended beyond their industries, as they began to invest in shaping societies through philanthropy, media, and political donations. They spearheaded initiatives aimed at addressing global challenges like climate change, education, and healthcare, often filling the gaps left by governments. Their actions were not merely altruistic; they understood that a stable, prosperous world was beneficial for their business interests. Consequently, their influence grew, fostering both admiration and skepticism among the global populace.

However, this newfound power was not without controversy. Critics argued that the concentration of wealth and influence in the hands of a few threatened democratic principles and exacerbated social inequalities. Questions arose about accountability, transparency, and the ethical implications of their involvement in public affairs. This chapter examines the intricate dynamics of how these economic titans emerged and the multifaceted impact of their ascendancy on global governance and societal structures.

2

Chapter 2: Sovereign States and Economic Sovereignty

The rise of billionaire influence did not occur in a vacuum; sovereign states played a pivotal role in shaping and responding to this phenomenon. As economic powerhouses, countries navigated the complexities of maintaining economic sovereignty while engaging with these influential private actors. Governments grappled with the challenge of regulating industries dominated by billionaires without stifling innovation or economic growth. This delicate balance required a nuanced understanding of economic policies and a strategic approach to diplomacy.

Countries like the United States, China, and India found themselves at the forefront of this new dynamic, each adopting distinct strategies to leverage the power of billionaires for national interests. The United States, with its liberal economic policies, fostered an environment conducive to the growth of tech giants and financial moguls. China, on the other hand, maintained a more controlled approach, balancing state intervention with market-driven growth. India's burgeoning tech industry showcased the potential for billionaires to drive economic development in emerging markets.

The relationship between states and billionaires was not merely economic; it encompassed geopolitical dimensions as well. These influential individuals often acted as informal diplomats, leveraging their global networks to facilitate international trade and negotiations. Their involvement in global forums, such as the World Economic Forum, underscored the symbiotic relationship between private wealth and public power. This chapter delves into the intricate interplay between sovereign states and billionaire influence, highlighting the strategies and implications of this evolving dynamic.

3

Chapter 3: The Digital Revolution and Global Connectivity

The digital revolution, driven by technological advancements and the proliferation of the internet, played a crucial role in shaping the new world order. Billionaires at the helm of tech giants like Apple, Microsoft, and Alibaba harnessed the power of innovation to connect the world in unprecedented ways. The rapid expansion of digital infrastructure facilitated global communication, commerce, and information exchange, transforming societies and economies alike.

This era of global connectivity ushered in new opportunities and challenges. On one hand, it democratized access to information and created new avenues for economic growth and social development. On the other hand, it raised concerns about data privacy, cybersecurity, and the monopolistic tendencies of tech giants. The influence of billionaires in the tech industry extended beyond business, as they became key players in shaping digital policies and governance frameworks.

The digital revolution also highlighted the importance of cross-border collaboration and the need for a cohesive approach to addressing global challenges. Billionaires, with their vast resources and global reach, emerged as influential advocates for issues such as internet governance, digital rights, and cyber resilience. Their involvement in multilateral initiatives underscored the need for a coordinated response to the complex challenges of the digital age. This chapter explores the transformative impact of the digital revolution on global connectivity and the role of billionaires in navigating this new frontier.

4

Chapter 4: Philanthropy and Global Impact

Philanthropy emerged as a powerful tool for billionaires to drive social change and address pressing global challenges. Through their charitable foundations and initiatives, they invested in areas such as education, healthcare, environmental conservation, and poverty alleviation. Their approach to philanthropy was often strategic, focusing on scalable solutions and measurable outcomes. This shift from traditional charitable giving to impact-driven philanthropy marked a significant evolution in how societal problems were addressed.

The influence of billionaire philanthropy extended beyond financial contributions. These individuals brought their business acumen, innovative thinking, and global networks to the philanthropic sector, fostering collaborations with governments, NGOs, and other stakeholders. Their initiatives often served as catalysts for systemic change, addressing root causes rather than mere symptoms. The Bill and Melinda Gates Foundation, for instance, played a pivotal role in global health initiatives, contributing to the eradication of diseases like polio and malaria.

However, billionaire philanthropy was not without its critics. Concerns about the accountability, transparency, and ethical implications of their involvement in public affairs persisted. Critics argued that the concentration of philanthropic power in the hands of a few undermined democratic principles and perpetuated existing inequalities. This chapter examines the multifaceted impact of billionaire philanthropy on global development and the ongoing debates surrounding its role in shaping the future of societies.

5

Chapter 5: The Influence of Media Moguls

Media moguls, with their vast empires encompassing television, print, and digital platforms, wielded significant influence over public opinion and discourse. Billionaires like Rupert Murdoch, Jeff Bezos, and Michael Bloomberg leveraged their media holdings to shape narratives, drive agendas, and influence political outcomes. The concentration of media ownership in the hands of a few raised important questions about the role of the press in democratic societies and the potential for conflicts of interest.

The influence of media moguls extended beyond traditional journalism. They recognized the power of digital platforms and social media in shaping public discourse and invested heavily in these areas. This shift towards digital media transformed the landscape of news consumption, with algorithms and data analytics playing a crucial role in content delivery. The rise of social media influencers and citizen journalism further democratized the dissemination of information, but also introduced challenges related to misinformation and echo chambers.

The role of media moguls in shaping public perception was not limited to domestic affairs; their influence extended to the global stage. They played a pivotal role in international diplomacy, using their platforms to advocate for issues such as human rights, climate change, and economic development. This chapter explores the complex dynamics of media ownership, the influence of billionaire media moguls, and the implications for democracy and global governance.

6

Chapter 6: Environmental Stewardship and Sustainability

As the world grappled with the existential threat of climate change, billionaires emerged as key players in the push for environmental sustainability. Through their investments in clean energy, conservation projects, and sustainable practices, they sought to mitigate the impact of climate change and promote a greener future. Their efforts were often aligned with broader global initiatives, such as the Paris Agreement and the United Nations Sustainable Development Goals.

Billionaires like Elon Musk, with his vision for electric vehicles and renewable energy, and Jeff Bezos, with his Earth Fund, exemplified the potential for private sector leadership in addressing environmental challenges. Their investments in innovation and technology drove significant advancements in areas such as electric mobility, carbon capture, and sustainable agriculture. These initiatives not only contributed to environmental sustainability but also created new economic opportunities and jobs.

However, the role of billionaires in environmental stewardship was met with both praise and criticism. Supporters lauded their contributions to sustainable development and their ability to drive systemic change. Critics, on the other hand, questioned the motivations behind their actions and the potential for greenwashing. This chapter delves into the intricate dynamics of billionaire-driven environmental initiatives, the challenges they face, and their impact on the global sustainability agenda.

7

Chapter 7: The Future of Global Governance

The evolving influence of billionaires on global affairs raised important questions about the future of global governance. As these individuals wielded significant economic and political power, their involvement in shaping international policies and institutions became more pronounced. Their participation in forums such as the World Economic Forum and the G7 underscored their role as informal diplomats and influencers of global agendas.

The influence of billionaires on global governance extended to areas such as trade, finance, and technology. Their expertise and resources enabled them to address complex challenges and drive innovative solutions. However, their involvement also highlighted the need for greater accountability and transparency in global decision-making processes. The interplay between state actors, international organizations, and influential individuals necessitated a reevaluation of existing governance frameworks.

The future of global governance hinged on the ability to balance the interests of diverse stakeholders and ensure inclusive and equitable decision-making. This chapter explores the implications of billionaire influence on global governance, the potential for new models of collaboration, and the challenges of maintaining democratic principles in an increasingly interconnected world.

8

Chapter 8: The Role of Financial Powerhouses

Financial powerhouses, including investment firms, banks, and hedge funds, played a crucial role in shaping the global economic landscape. Billionaires at the helm of these institutions, such as Warren Buffett and Larry Fink, wielded significant influence over capital markets, corporate governance, and economic policies. Their investment decisions had far-reaching implications for industries, economies, and societies.

The influence of financial powerhouses extended beyond traditional finance. They embraced new investment strategies, such as impact investing and ESG (environmental, social, and governance) criteria, to drive positive social and environmental outcomes. Their focus on sustainable investing reflected a growing recognition of the interconnectedness of financial performance and societal well-being. This shift towards responsible investing marked a significant evolution in the financial sector.

However, the concentration of financial power in the hands of a few raised concerns about market manipulation, economic stability, and regulatory oversight. The influence of financial billionaires extended to political donations and lobbying, further blurring the lines between private interests and public policy. This chapter examines the role of financial powerhouses in shaping global economic trends, the evolution of responsible investing, and the challenges of ensuring transparency and accountability in the financial sector.

9

Chapter 9: Health and Biotechnology Innovations

The intersection of wealth and biotechnology marked a new frontier in healthcare innovation. Billionaires like Bill Gates, with his focus on global health initiatives, and biotech pioneers such as Patrick Soon-Shiong, leveraged their resources to drive advancements in medical research, treatments, and technologies. Their investments in biotechnology promised breakthroughs in areas such as genomics, personalized medicine, and disease eradication.

The influence of billionaire-driven healthcare initiatives extended to global health challenges, such as pandemics and neglected tropical diseases. Their contributions to vaccine development, healthcare infrastructure, and public health campaigns played a pivotal role in addressing health disparities and improving access to quality care. The COVID-19 pandemic, in particular, underscored the importance of coordinated efforts and the potential for private sector leadership in crisis response.

However, the involvement of billionaires in healthcare also raised ethical considerations and debates about the commercialization of medical research. Concerns about data privacy, equitable access to treatments, and the influence of profit motives on healthcare priorities persisted. This chapter explores the transformative impact of billionaire-driven health and biotechnology innovations, the ethical implications, and the potential for future advancements in the field.

10

Chapter 10: Education and Knowledge Economy

Education emerged as a critical area of focus for billionaires seeking to drive social change and economic development. Through their philanthropic efforts, they invested in initiatives aimed at improving educational access, quality, and equity. Billionaires like Mark Zuckerberg, with his emphasis on personalized learning, and Laurene Powell Jobs, with her focus on innovative education models, exemplified the potential for private sector contributions to the knowledge economy.

The influence of billionaire-driven education initiatives extended to areas such as curriculum development, teacher training, and digital learning platforms. Their investments in technology-enabled education aimed to bridge the digital divide and provide students with the skills needed for the future workforce. The COVID-19 pandemic accelerated the adoption of online learning, highlighting the importance of digital infrastructure and equitable access to education.

However, the role of billionaires in education also sparked debates about the privatization of public education and the potential for inequities in access and outcomes. Critics argued that the concentration of philanthropic power in education decision-making could undermine democratic principles and perpetuate existing disparities. This chapter delves into the impact of billionaire-driven education initiatives, the challenges of ensuring equitable access, and the potential for innovation in the knowledge economy.

11

Chapter 11: Cultural and Creative Industries

Billionaires played a significant role in shaping the cultural and creative industries, leveraging their resources to support the arts, entertainment, and media. Through their patronage and investments, they contributed to the growth and sustainability of cultural institutions, creative projects, and artistic endeavors. Billionaires like David Geffen, with his contributions to the music and film industries, and François Pinault, with his investments in contemporary art, exemplified the potential for private sector support in the cultural sphere.

The influence of billionaires in the cultural and creative industries extended to areas such as museum funding, film production, and digital content creation. Their involvement often facilitated the preservation of cultural heritage, the promotion of artistic expression, and the dissemination of creative works. The rise of digital platforms further transformed the landscape of cultural consumption, enabling global access to diverse forms of artistic content.

However, the role of billionaires in the cultural sector also raised questions about the commercialization of art and the potential for market-driven influences on artistic expression. Concerns about the concentration of cultural power and the impact on artistic diversity and independence persisted. This chapter explores the impact of billionaire-driven support for the cultural and creative industries, the challenges of balancing commercial and artistic interests, and the potential for future innovations in the cultural sphere.

12

Chapter 12: Space Exploration and the Final Frontier

The quest for space exploration, once the exclusive domain of governments, witnessed a new era of private sector involvement, driven by billionaire entrepreneurs. Visionaries like Elon Musk, with SpaceX, and Jeff Bezos, with Blue Origin, embarked on ambitious missions to explore the final frontier, aiming to revolutionize space travel and establish human presence beyond Earth. Their investments in space technology and exploration marked a significant shift in the aerospace industry.

The influence of billionaire-driven space initiatives extended to areas such as satellite technology, space tourism, and interplanetary colonization. Their efforts promised advancements in space research, communication infrastructure, and the potential for economic opportunities in space. The vision of a multi-planetary future captured the imagination of the global populace and underscored the potential for private sector leadership in space exploration.

However, the involvement of billionaires in space exploration also raised ethical and regulatory considerations. Concerns about space debris, the militarization of space, and the equitable access to space resources emerged as important issues. The collaboration between private and public sectors became crucial in addressing these challenges and ensuring the responsible exploration of the final frontier. This chapter delves into the transformative impact of billionaire-driven space initiatives, the challenges they face, and the potential for future exploration and innovation in space.

13

Chapter 13: The Intersection of Technology and Human Rights

The rise of billionaires in the tech industry brought about significant advancements in technology, but also raised important questions about human rights and ethical considerations. The influence of tech giants on issues such as data privacy, digital rights, and artificial intelligence highlighted the need for a balance between innovation and ethical responsibility. Billionaires like Tim Cook, with his advocacy for privacy, and Sundar Pichai, with his focus on AI ethics, exemplified the potential for tech leadership in addressing human rights concerns.

The impact of technology on human rights extended to areas such as surveillance, freedom of expression, and access to information. The role of social media platforms in shaping public discourse and the challenges of content moderation and misinformation underscored the complexities of tech governance. The involvement of billionaires in shaping digital policies and ethical frameworks became crucial in navigating these challenges.

However, the concentration of tech power in the hands of a few raised concerns about accountability, transparency, and the potential for abuse of power. The need for robust regulatory frameworks and multi-stakeholder collaborations became apparent in addressing these issues. This chapter explores the intersection of technology and human rights, the role of billionaire tech leaders in shaping ethical considerations, and the challenges of ensuring a rights-respecting digital future.

14

Chapter 14: Global Health Crises and Pandemic Preparedness

The COVID-19 pandemic underscored the importance of global health preparedness and the role of billionaires in crisis response. Billionaires like Bill Gates, with his focus on pandemic preparedness and vaccine development, played a pivotal role in addressing the health crisis. Their contributions to research, healthcare infrastructure, and public health campaigns highlighted the potential for private sector leadership in global health.

The influence of billionaires in pandemic response extended to areas such as vaccine distribution, public health education, and healthcare access. Their efforts to support healthcare systems, particularly in low- and middle-income countries, underscored the importance of equitable access to healthcare resources. The collaboration between private and public sectors became crucial in addressing the global health crisis.

However, the role of billionaires in pandemic preparedness also raised ethical and logistical considerations. Concerns about the equitable distribution of vaccines, the transparency of funding allocations, and the potential for conflicts of interest emerged as important issues. This chapter delves into the impact of billionaire-driven efforts in global health crises, the challenges of ensuring equitable access and preparedness, and the potential for future collaborations in global health.

15

Chapter 15: The Power of Social Movements

Social movements, driven by grassroots activism and advocacy, played a crucial role in shaping the global landscape. Billionaires, recognizing the importance of social change, invested in initiatives aimed at supporting and amplifying social movements. Their contributions to causes such as racial justice, gender equality, and LGBTQ+ rights exemplified the potential for private sector support in driving social change.

The influence of billionaires in social movements extended to areas such as funding advocacy organizations, supporting policy reforms, and leveraging media platforms to raise awareness. Their involvement often facilitated the amplification of marginalized voices and the promotion of social justice initiatives. The collaboration between philanthropists and activists highlighted the potential for transformative social change.

However, the role of billionaires in social movements also sparked debates about the authenticity and motivations behind their involvement. Concerns about the co-optation of social movements and the potential for philanthropic influence on grassroots activism emerged as important issues. This chapter explores the impact of billionaire-driven support for social movements, the challenges of maintaining authenticity and accountability, and the potential for future collaborations in driving social change.

16

Chapter 16: The Future of Work and Economic Inclusion

The rapid advancements in technology and automation transformed the future of work and raised important questions about economic inclusion. Billionaires, with their investments in innovation and workforce development, played a pivotal role in shaping the future of work. Their contributions to areas such as reskilling, entrepreneurship, and inclusive economic growth highlighted the potential for private sector leadership in addressing workforce challenges.

The influence of billionaires in the future of work extended to areas such as digital platforms, gig economy, and remote work. Their investments in technology-enabled solutions aimed to bridge the skills gap and provide workers with the tools needed for the evolving job market. The focus on economic inclusion reflected a growing recognition of the interconnectedness of workforce development and societal well-being.

However, the role of billionaires in the future of work also raised concerns about job displacement, labor rights, and the potential for economic inequalities. The need for robust policies and collaborative efforts became apparent in addressing these challenges and ensuring a just and inclusive future of work. This chapter delves into the impact of billionaire-driven initiatives on the future of work, the challenges of economic inclusion, and the potential for innovation in workforce development.

17

Chapter 17: Charting a New Course for the Global Future

As we move forward into the mid-21st century, the intertwined influences of billionaires and sovereign states continue to shape the global order. Their roles in driving technological advancements, economic growth, and social change underscore the complexities and possibilities of our interconnected world. Billionaires, with their resources and innovative thinking, offer the potential for significant contributions to global challenges, yet their influence necessitates careful scrutiny and regulation.

The future of the global order will hinge on the ability to balance private interests with public welfare, ensuring that the benefits of innovation and economic growth are equitably distributed. Collaboration between billionaires, governments, and international organizations will be essential in addressing issues such as climate change, economic inequality, and global health crises. The interplay between private wealth and public power will continue to evolve, requiring adaptive governance frameworks and a commitment to transparency and accountability.

Ultimately, the blueprint for a new world order will be shaped by the collective efforts of diverse stakeholders, driven by a shared vision of a just, sustainable, and prosperous future. This chapter concludes with a reflection

CHAPTER 17: CHARTING A NEW COURSE FOR THE GLOBAL FUTURE

on the lessons learned from the rise of billionaires and their impact on global governance, highlighting the potential for a more inclusive and equitable world.

18

Epilogue: The Legacy of the Global Architects

The legacy of the global architects, comprised of billionaires and countries, will be defined by their contributions to shaping the future of our world. Their influence on economic policies, technological advancements, and social initiatives underscores the transformative potential of private sector leadership. However, their legacy will also be marked by the challenges and debates surrounding their involvement in public affairs and the ethical considerations of their actions.

As we navigate the complexities of the 21st century, the lessons learned from the rise of billionaires and their impact on global governance will inform future strategies for collaboration and innovation. The ongoing dialogue between private and public sectors will be crucial in addressing global challenges and ensuring a more equitable and sustainable world.

The story of the global architects is one of ambition, innovation, and influence. It is a testament to the power of visionary leadership and the potential for collective action in shaping the future. As we look to the future, the legacy of these influential individuals and their contributions to the global order will continue to inspire and challenge us to strive for a better world.

The Global Architects: Billionaires, Countries, and the Blueprint for a New World Order

EPILOGUE: THE LEGACY OF THE GLOBAL ARCHITECTS

In an era marked by unprecedented wealth and influence, "The Global Architects" delves into the intricate web of power dynamics between billionaires and sovereign states. This thought-provoking book explores how these economic titans and influential countries shape the global order, blending economic might with geopolitical strategy to forge a new blueprint for the future.

Through seventeen insightful chapters, the book examines the rise of billionaires, their philanthropic endeavors, and their impact on technology, media, and global health. It highlights their role in shaping public opinion, driving social movements, and pioneering space exploration. Simultaneously, it underscores the delicate balance that sovereign states must maintain in regulating these influential actors while fostering innovation and economic growth.

"The Global Architects" offers a comprehensive analysis of the evolving relationship between private wealth and public power, addressing ethical considerations, accountability, and the quest for a more equitable and sustainable world. It provides readers with a nuanced understanding of the complex interplay between billionaires and countries, ultimately charting a course for the future of global governance and economic inclusion.

This book is a must-read for anyone interested in the transformative potential of private sector leadership, the challenges of modern governance, and the quest for a just and prosperous world.

www.ingramcontent.com/pod-product-compliance
Lightning Source LLC
LaVergne TN
LVHW010441070526
838199LV00066B/6132